Dear Spanish

Dear Spanish
poems

Mateo Acuña

Copyright © 2024 by Mateo Acuña
Cover Art by Mateo Acuña

All rights reserved. No part of this publication may be reproduced, distributed, or transmitted in any form or by any means, including photocopying, recording, or other electronic or mechanical methods, without the prior written permission of the author, except in the case of brief quotations embodied in critical reviews and certain other noncommercial uses permitted by copyright law.

The Seattle Youth Poet Laureate is a special program of
Seattle Arts & Lectures in partnership with Urban Word.

ISBN 978-1-949166-09-5

Published by Poetry NW Editions
2000 Tower Street
Everett, WA 98201

Distributed by Ingram

PRINTED IN THE UNITED STATES OF AMERICA

Contents

The Story of the Scar on My Left Knee — 1

Renaissance — 2

The Bind — 3

Artist's Bracket — 4

Ode to Sertraline — 5

To the Fledgling Thrush — 6

Ode to the Coyote — 8

Sagrada Família — 11

My Testimony — 12

The Poet at Seventeen — 13

My Father: — 15

Dear Spanish, — 16

Querido español, — 17

Meditation on Belonging — 18

America Lives a Fantasy — 19

Spanish Moss — 20

Working Men — 21

Trickle-Down — 23

Someday — 24

Dear Salish Sea, — 25

La Cosa con Plumas — 26

Acknowledgments — 27

Notes — 28

About the Author — 29

The Story of the Scar on My Left Knee

At eighteen, I rode a moped on the dirt trails of el Valle Sagrado,
said buenas tardes to the rainbow-woven people,
wondered if that was how
my ancestors lived before they moved
out of the jungle, changed their native surname Tantayatas

to the Spanish Tantalleón, exchanged their tongues
for the conquerors' and passed it abajo, abajo,
down to me. I could barely
fit it in my American mouth,
grinning like the moon as the wheels spun
faster, faster, más rápido until—hasta, I was speeding

downhill like a snowball picking up snow, helpless
to physics, helpless to fate, helpless, helpless
to the speed bump made of dirt road
because the government
keeps its money in pockets with holes.
When I saw it, two choices presented themselves

like the two faces of Pachakamaq, both violent
and ill-ending. I chose to veer,
flinging my body
off the bike, teeth scraping
the turquoise-stoned sky, bones breaking
into feathers like the third Ayar brother, eyes blinded

from the gaze of Inti, mind bodiless for but a moment
in which gravity, time, and reason left,
earth's axis stopped turning, language ceased—

before landing on one knee with my hands
in the dirt as just another breathing
thing among the dust and rocks.

Renaissance

My friends and I went on a Sunday morning, nerds' church.
Cars full of fairies and mermaids, witches and wizards,
pirates and merchants, royals and peasants, lined the exit
for miles like a cavalcade, then were left in a lot to burn

under the magnifying glass sun. We walked through
the facade of a stone castle into the English Renaissance
resurrected—a mass of tents nailed into a dirt lot,
flat as a playing card. The crowds kicked up swirls

of dust that coated the vendors' merchandise as if it had
sat for ages in a ship or a cell: leather cuffs, corsets,
swords, animal horns made into music instruments,
and hand-hammered jewelry. In the back, striped tents spooled long lines

for cotton candy and ice cream floats, nachos and gyros,
turkey legs and chicken fingers, beer and sarsaparilla.
We ate overpriced and under-toppinged nachos, learned
to throw axes at the rings of tree trunks and split time,

watched jousting on horses, dancers, and a play,
then walked the paths languidly with sore feet,
dirt-dusted shoes and hair, and drained wallets.
We passed a grassy fenced area with an arched trellis,

a mini portcullis missing its bite, flanked by two white
men dressed head-to-toe in knight's armor. The sign
on the trellis read *The Spanish Court*. Suddenly
I was in my skin again because the white men

were in their skin again. The olive-green tunic
I'd bought for forty bucks now felt cheap as shillings,
like the tents with their merchandise, the food, the music—
all of it a shrine wrapped in armor and made shiny,

made fun, made easy to wear the outfit and forget
who sewed it, to eat the food and forget who cooked it,
to praise the pillar and forget its shadow, to forget
that for a Renaissance to take place, something had to die.

The Bind

I wrap my breasts in shadow;
flatten them like dried pansies
between the pages of a book.

Artist's Bracket

When I cut my hair, I smash a record, fracture a song,
rip pages from a calendar, chop down a tree, and leave a stump.
When I cut my hair, I need three mirrors: one in front of me,
one behind me, and one beside me. As the minutes stretch
into hours, I become trapped in mirrors, learn to move
in their realm, inverse: up is down, right is left,
forward is backward. I bring the whirring blades
around my ears that grow like shelf fungi.
Once I used a twelve-foot-tall fallen sapling
to knock down a hefty piece of artist's bracket
that grew like a frog's pouch mouth on the side of an evergreen.
Dopamine hit when it fell. It fogged up the sandwich bag
with its breath like a kid huffing at a cold winter window.
It sat on my kitchen island for days before I threw it away—
a destructive, useless conquest. A surgeon cut out
my uterus and threw it away. I never saw that hockey puck
of an organ I had growing inside me. If it were mine,
I would have dressed it in the long strands of hair
I snipped and given my father the girl he wanted.

Ode to Sertraline

Every morning, the choice rests in the center of my palm
between the head line and the life line: a fat sprinkle
sweating off its smoky blue film from my heat,
painting my insides on what was supposed to be my shell.

One face is imprinted with two letters divided by
a scored middle, their meanings unknown,
or for the illusion of meaning. To me,
they stand for "Inherent Grievance," each on either side

of a valley made for teeth to bite, where my father
and mother collide, together and separate,
where my siblings and I reside. The hidden face
ranks our anxiety in birth order, 213.

It's a painting of each of us in a line, heads bent,
chasing each other's endings like a run-on sentence,
like when I pick up my prescription and the pharmacist says
would you like to pick up your sister's as well

and hands me a brown paper bag shrouding
sprinkles the color of a cloudless sky,
each original feeling clinking against
the other in the neon polypropylene tube.

To the Fledgling Thrush

panting in the heat of the hottest summer on record,
stranded for hours in a tangle of leaves and brush,
flapping your wings, flightless, in fear of the four
beings towering above you. To your speckled body

that wriggled in the gray hoodie where I held you
with cupped hands, to the tufts of downy feathers
that sprouted from your head like owl ears, to your
round, red belly, snapping yellow beak, and chirps—

we called wildlife sanctuaries. None of them took
birds. They said not to touch you. They said some
are born to die, that nature finds a way to survive.
They said now there is a line where trees become

concrete, trails become drive-thrus, and birdsongs
become telephone wires. Where rivers become bottles
of water mixed with salt to keep us thirsty.
But on the walk through the wetlands before we found you,

we saw socks in the dirt, plastic cups and chip wrappers
in the deep sink peat bog, and a shoe hiking to nowhere
on its side under a bush. We saw smoky polypores
decomposing freshly fallen trees.

Their clean insides looked like IKEA wood.
We stepped aside for motorcyclists to pass and choked
on their gas smoke as they laughed past a solitary water
lily floating on its own reflection. We heard an owl call

from far above then a siren wail from 4th Avenue.
At the end of one path, we were greeted by a Porta Potty
that smelled like it was leaking, a gravel lot, a 7-Eleven,
and a log cabin that was once a real estate office to sell

stolen land. It overlooked a lake where we stopped
to watch birds playing or mating or fighting;
it was impossible to tell, but it looked like paradise.
A cardinal meadowhawk landed on a piece of wood

protruding from the water and flexed its transparent
red-veined wings, basking in the sun as if it were posing
for us, as if all the birds were out for us, as if the sun shone
for us. I took pictures, but not of the gravel lot or the shoe

or the wrappers, or of you. Because I left you in the bush
and drove away and ate liquid nitrogen ice cream and reveled
at the way it stuck to my tongue like how the memory
of you has stuck to me, even after you have melted away.

Ode to the Coyote

Tan skin, tan voice,
square jaw, and white shirt
pulled taut, a posture

of abstinence. Knots
of muscle, broad shoulders,
tight hips, slender legs—

in high school they called him
Coyote because he was so
skinny. Now my father calls

himself a gym rat, fighting
to get back that slimness,
fighting to fill the quiet

where the gnawing
enters with the *wish*
of weights sliding

onto the barbell, fighting
age with diet and exercise
and secrets. Coyote

is a trickster who fools
the eye, who makes you
believe he could never die.

Coyote told the first lie.
But his slippery tongue
ran off, let loose, and knotted

itself a noose
no language could untangle,
because a coyote is a coyote,

the same in English and Spanish,
a perfect cognate. But understand this:
there could be no heroes

nor villains, no beginnings nor
endings, no happiness nor sorrows,
without a Coyote.

My father and I break bread
over this word because it cannot
become lost in translation

like so many others. We eat guiso
de papa, sudado pescado, and
tallarines rojos over this word.

We toast with chicha morada,
maracuyá, and Inca Kola over
this word. For twenty years

we have sliced panettone on
New Year's with this word,
our bridge from Trujillo, Peru,

to Auburn, Washington, from
booming waves of terra-cotta
roofs and tangled telephone

wires to dark forests and angled
houses huddled close around the heat
of the railroad. Here, electricity

travels underground, buzzes
beneath the concrete, the little
shake in our tires, the pep in our

step, the caffeine in our veins. Here,
coyotes howl at the witching hour
like a crowd of crying babies, from

the swamp hills across the valley
to the farmland laced with electricity
pylons like paper chains of pancaked

Eiffel Towers where he's resided since
she left him, waiting for a spark
that could only cause a fire.

As a child, he watched cartoons
from morning to noon, just him
and the screen, Wile E. Coyote

chasing after the Road Runner
again and again and again—
and every day, I pass a coyote

lying on its side by the side
of the freeway just before Golden
Given Road, facing away from

passing cars. It has been rotting
there for three weeks in the stench of paper
sulfur, oil, and its own flesh, in long

puddles broken up by grooved cement
mirroring the sky above, cerulean smoked
puffs of white. Three weeks, and no one

has come to bury it. Again and again
and again I look in the rearview mirror,
but I can't see its expression.

Sagrada Família

I realized my obsession with Sagrada Família—a motley
of cultures, expressions, dreams, and spoils sewn together
into an architectural patchwork quilt—was less about me
and more about the family I grew up in.

To Latinos and Mormons, the family unit is impenetrable
and sacred. Like the cathedral's construction, we ran, walked,
inched, then petered perpetually towards wholeness in Zeno's
dichotomy paradox, never quite able to reach the end.

We kept halving ourselves in service of the whole before
we knew exactly what we were giving up, because my father
was the architect and he was never satisfied. He drew
and redrew the lines. And since I was young I could see

the faint etchings of where he drew and redrew the finish line,
a little further away each time. I grew up angry. When I was older,
I realized he was redrawing it in his sleep. And while all of us had
halved ourselves over and over and over, he had halved himself

for longer, still halves himself, even when now all he has
is himself, a granule of graphite so close to nothing, to perfect.
The rest of his halves are in the vault, figures in the dark
that move when they think no one's watching.

My Testimony

I don't remember how or when I was gifted ten dollars,
a rare occurrence for me growing up, but come Sunday,
my parents made me give ten percent of it as tithing
to the Mormon Church, the way my father did his wages,
the way everyone in the Church did their income.
The blow was devastating. The blow was ten cents.
I had planned on buying two LPS, or Littlest Pet Shops,
bug-eyed animal bobbleheads that could fit in the palm
of my hand. They were exactly five dollars each
and collected by little girls everywhere. My friends always
had more of them than I did. Now my dollar went
not to a second LPS, but to the LDS, a very different
kind of cult. Now my dollar funded a mall in Utah
or a priest's Ferrari. At eight, I was baptized
jacuzzi-style, leaving the sins I presumably had
with my seven-year-old self, making room
for the many more to come. After I changed
out of the heavy white robe and dried off,
the priest had me join the audience, which felt wrong,
since I thought I was the star. The chairs were metal,
collapsible, the color of dust, "LDS" spray-painted
in white block, militaristic letters as if they had been tagged
by a gang of religious zealots. The priest stood at the head
of the room behind a podium and said a prayer.
I opened my eyes in the middle of it and looked around.
Surely, if I were to see Him, it would be now;
Jesus was ruggedly handsome, with flowing auburn hair,
a full, luscious beard; mirror-gray eyes; and pale pink skin,
according to the famous Mormon portrait. If mortal eyes
were too weak to see him in his full hunk form,
I was told he would appear like a mass of light. Alas,
Jesus was a no-show. Still, I believed in Him
like I did the ghost of the old woman who died
decades ago in our house, who my father saw
as a shadow on the wall crossing his room at night,
who I saw as a middle-aged woman watching me in the corner
of the kitchen in the corner of my eye, disappearing
whenever I looked directly.

The Poet at Seventeen

didn't exist. There was only her, the girl who will go
unnamed, who keeps chasing me, who keeps screaming
that she's my skeleton, that I'm dead and she's me.
I changed my name but somehow she found me

and fills my mailbox with letters addressed to me
as herself. I moved to a new house in a new city
and she followed me. She goes digging in my backyard,
unearthing zombies and telling them to call me by her name.

When she died, she left her belongings in my house,
girly things I have no use for: makeup, crop tops, skirts,
long haircuts, breasts, ovaries, menstrual cycles, and memories
of straight ex-boyfriends she hides around the house like

jump scares and gives to the monster under my bed as fodder
for blackmail. She appears in my mirrors, computer screens,
family photo albums, closets, shadowy corners late at night,
in the center of the room on the sunniest day, and settings on my phone

I can't change. She lived in my body and passed it off
as her own for years, sculpting my face with feathery blades,
distorting my figure with estrogen, bras, belts,
and feminine jeans, the two kisses on each cheek

before she pushed me backwards into a cellar and slammed
the trapdoor shut. The light was thin. She forgot me
for years at a time. I scratched stories like tally marks
on the cement walls and wrote characters brave enough to speak

where I fell silent. When the world shut down,
she rendered me on her face like a police sketch artist,
drawing me out of murky details. When she looked
in the mirror, I looked back. The world made horrible sense.

She saw she was not real, but a construction of others'
desires. My mother saw me and told me to wipe me away.
I did not. I remained the next day and the day after that
until the days piled into weeks. Everyday I cried

because in the time I had been away my body
sweared loyalty to her. Now my chest was too large,
my hips too wide, my voice too high to convince anyone
that I was a boy, even my parents. My father cornered me

and asked me if I wanted to be a boy. He said it so
angrily, like a threat, that I said no. I was wearing
overalls with rainbow straps and everything about me
was a target. Every day felt like the end of the world.

I had no masculine clothes and no money to buy any.
I asked for a short haircut at the salon, and they made
a choppy mess that looked like a mistake.
Too long, too short, I turned it into a bob with bangs

and gave my misshapen body back to her. She cast me out
to the vanishing point, as far as the mind could see,
and continued on as if nothing had happened,
celebrating her eighteenth birthday without me.

My Father:

I ▮▮▮▮▮▮▮▮▮▮▮▮▮▮▮▮
▮▮▮▮ in guilt I was born, ▮▮▮▮
▮▮▮▮▮▮▮▮▮▮▮▮▮▮▮▮

II ▮▮▮▮ you love ▮▮▮▮
▮▮▮▮ the secret ▮▮▮▮
▮▮▮▮▮▮▮▮▮▮▮▮▮▮▮▮

Antiphon

I Make me ▮▮▮▮▮▮▮▮
▮▮▮▮▮▮▮▮▮▮▮▮▮▮▮▮
▮▮▮▮ turn away from your face
▮▮▮▮▮▮▮▮▮▮

II ▮▮▮▮▮▮▮▮▮▮▮▮▮▮▮▮
▮▮ cast me away from your presence,
▮▮▮▮▮▮▮▮▮▮▮▮▮▮▮▮
▮▮▮▮ deprive me of you ▮▮▮▮

I Give me again ▮ joy ▮▮▮▮
▮▮▮▮ a spirit ▮▮▮▮
▮▮▮▮ trans▮▮▮▮
▮▮▮▮ sinner ▮▮▮▮ to you.

II ▮▮▮▮▮▮▮▮▮▮▮▮▮▮▮▮
▮▮▮▮▮▮▮▮▮▮▮▮▮▮▮▮
▮▮▮▮ <u>open</u> my lips
and my mouth shall de<u>clare</u> ▮▮▮▮

I ▮▮▮▮ take ▮ delight
▮▮▮▮ from ▮▮▮▮
my ▮▮▮▮ spirit ▮▮▮▮
▮▮▮▮▮▮▮▮▮▮▮▮▮▮▮▮

Dear Spanish,

Hello old friend. Have you stopped hiding from me? Have you stopped pretending that you're listening just around the corner, is that why you touch me with silence? Or is it because two worlds are tearing me apart and I don't have enough native in the blood of my mouth to give you as a sacrifice?

You of all people know best that everything in life is a transaction. If I gave you what I know of Quechua, would you give me the same words in Spanish? All I ask is that you make me complete, that you be the missing piece, that you be the cement to fill the potholes of memories in which I felt outside of something that was supposed to be part of me.

I don't want to see you as my father anymore. He was never the key to the mentality of an entire language, of an entire country. Do you know what it feels like to love a country that doesn't love you back? In a way, you and I are the same. We both want to live in places where we don't belong. But the difference is that even though I try to be your friend, you are the reason why I will always be an exile from my second home.

Spanish, the truth is that I am writing to you because I am in love with you like a festering wound that asks for a scab. I know that I am suffering because of you, that I may never return to Peru because of you, but my skin will always be the color of my desire for you. I long to explore every curve and crevice of your body, savor the sweat of your labor, the tears of my tanned-skinned ancestors, marvel at your cathedral of mottled architecture and see myself in the reflection of its stained-glass windows. Maybe then my expression will be so fractured by rainbows that it will start to look happy.

Querido español,

Hola viejo amigo. ¿Has dejado de esconderte de mí todavía? ¿Has dejado de fingir que estás escuchando a la vuelta de la esquina, es por eso que tocarme con silencio? ¿O es que dos mundos me están desgarrando y no tengo suficiente nativo en la sangre de mi boca para darte en sacrificio?

Usted de todas las personas sabe mejor que todo en la vida es una transacción. ¿Si te diera lo que sé de quechua, me darías las mismas palabras en tu lengua? Todo lo que te pido es que me hagas completo, que ser la pieza que falta, que ser cemento para llenar los baches de los recuerdos en los que me sentía fuera de algo que formaba parte de mí.

Ya no quiero verte como mi padre. Nunca fue el clave de la mentalidad de todo un idioma, de todo un país. ¿Sabes lo que se siente amar a un país que no te ama también? En cierto modo, tú y yo somos iguales. Ambos queremos vivir en lugares a los que no pertenecemos. Pero la diferencia es que, aunque trato de ser tu amigo, tú eres la razón por la siempre seré un exiliado de mi segunda casa.

Español, la verdad es que te escribo porque estoy enamorado de ti como una herida supurante que pide costra. Sé que por ti estoy sufriendo, que tal vez nunca regrese al Perú, pero mi piel siempre será del color de mi deseo por ti. Anhelo explorar cada curva y hendidura de saborear el sudor de tu trabajo, las lágrimas de mis ancestros de piel bronceada, maravillarme con tu catedral de arquitectura moteada y verme en el reflejo de los vitrales. Tal vez mi expresión está tan fracturada en arcoíris que comience a verse feliz.

Meditation on Belonging

Tranquilo, my father tells Uncle Wilson, unveiling a plunger
from a plastic Walmart bag, like a big black version
of the marbelized poppers I used to get from vending
machines as a kid, with a wood handle like a witch's
broom. I suck a laugh from my gut so he knows
I understand his Spanish, how I did with Uncle Carlos
and his family around the dinner table the night
my father and I landed in Lima. It was like the Peruvian
Last Supper hanging in Cathedral Basilica, except
we had chicken and fries instead of guinea pig
and wine, except I was dark Judas. I didn't know
half the jokes, I just wanted to be in on them,
didn't know half the people, just wanted to be like them
while I looked out of the frame at you and said,
See? Look at me. Look at us. At the end of my past life,
I was a girl in high school who couldn't see
herself in the mirror. I remember what it was like
to breathe in those halls, weed like skunk spray
wafting from bathroom stalls, Axe and Old Spice
underpinned with body odor and bad breath behind gum
smack and crap talk stuck behind beige chairs chained
to beige desks chained to beige walls chained to monochrome
clocks with faces that ticked us off and a red needle spinning
like a broken compass. I was so worried someone would hear me
breathing in the clockwork chaos, that everyone would realize
I was only human. I started to breathe shallow,
like I did at Pisac, Peru, 9,751 meters above sea level,
the summer after I graduated. When I was there,
a Latina tourist was taking a picture at the top,
under the blue bowl sky whipped with clouds,
the mountains venerated as apukana as her photo
backdrop. She was wearing an afterimage
of the kitschy *breathe* shirts in America, except
hers simply said, *breath*. I couldn't stop laughing.
No one else with me did, even after I explained it
to them, and how could they? They were all from Peru.

America Lives a Fantasy

America lives a fantasy so vivid,
so persuasive,

very much

Men look at women. Women watch them
look at

a
conception
invented so that a seventeen-year-
old boy would be likely to invent

a mother

Spanish Moss

Also known as tree hair or itla-okla,
hangs from branches like a beard tangled in pursuit,
as long as five hundred and thirty two years, long since
before that, when trees could just be trees,
moss could just be moss
and hair could just be hair.

Working Men

On a beautiful Tuesday morning in Seattle, sunny
not yet sweltering, a man lies across the sidewalk
on 10th Avenue like a speed bump. His head is in
a bush as if the branches are neural pathways,

each thought an almond-shaped leaf. He wears
no socks and different shoes on each foot.
Some of his belongings lie beside him,
including a matching shoe and a blowtorch.

His pants are too short, exposing ankles tanned
from life outdoors, ridden with eczema flaking
and splotching like in the crooks of my elbows
and knees, on my hands and fingers, around

my eyes and in the corners of my lips, and in that
I feel kinship with this man. But I have come
from a Polyclinic appointment and will have
a prescription ready after work and have work

while everyday for him is work to find what is
gifted to me. I wish for eczema cream
to set beside him. I wonder how many miles
his ankles have carried, how weary he must have

been to sleep on a mattress of concrete through clangs
and shouts from cross-hatched cranes like looms
spinning spindly sleek luxury apartments
poised at the end of the street like a supermodel

at the beginning of a runway. They're built so
their glassy exteriors reflect the cartoonish sitcom
optimism of the blue and cotton ball sky and not
the unhoused man unconscious or dead

in the construction walkway with the makeshift joint
clamped between his teeth that points like an unsheathed
sword at the fine white powder on a crinkly rectangle
of aluminum foil in his sooty brown hand.

Parts of the foil reflect the sunlight streaming into the walkway,
a blinding white winking iridescent. But the unshone folds
of the foil look like a mirror looking at a mirror looking
on and so forth, a sort of anxious insanity, a shiny, undefinable gray,

a space carved where there is no space,
a place displaced though there is no place.

Trickle-Down

I thought I grew up in poverty until I realized
I was only made to feel that way. Trickle-down
economics says cut taxes for the rich,
and their money will flow like wine
down a pyramid of goblets, filling first
their own, then cascading down,
                            down,
                                  down,
but any waiter could tell you that only makes a blood-
colored puddle and broken glass. When I was three,
my father had to take an economics class for his master's
in business, which he worked on in the evenings at home,
after work. At the start of the night, he'd go out
and buy a six-pack. When it was gone, he'd go out and buy
        a second. When that was gone, he'd go out and buy
                a third. As the night blurred,
                      the quality of his essay would go down,
                                              down,
                                                      down,
into something incomprehensible. In the morning, he'd ask my mother
to look over it. *Just for the grammar*, he'd say, since English was
his second language. But my mother had to read his textbooks
to learn the concepts to revise then rewrite the rest of the essay.
The degree was as much hers as it was his, but even after AA,
when beer became chocolate or hours on Facebook,
the money it brought in stayed in his goblet.

Someday

is bare-chested with swim trunks.
Waves of chlorine, sunlight, and synths lap
like a happy dog on my butterscotch skin.
No soggy sagging wire-wrought bikini top to ring out
and hang, just droplets that evaporate
and diffuse into the summer air.

Dear Salish Sea,

I wonder what you would think of us now. How we walk with our lips closed as tightly as the oysters you carry. How we blow smoke that turns your reflection to steel. We have learned coldness from your waters, have turned away from you as a source of strength.

You gladly swallow our bottle caps and plastic wraps, then lay them at our feet like humble offerings asking us to change. You used to be seen on a miles-long shore near my home. That shore has been reduced to a sanctioned square behind a chain-link fence downtown, hidden behind dizzying skyscrapers that cut the land like teeth through the gum.

You used to float otters. Now all you float is aimless driftwood I turn into deconstructed dreamcatchers. Like your receding shore, traditional knowledge of the craft left me behind in the hourglass of time. But in you I see the tenacity and resilience of my Chippewa foremothers showing me what it means to adapt. Your presence is hope. A love letter to the future.

La Cosa con Plumas

When I started calling myself a man, I first thought
teakwood, tobacco, mahogany, whiskey, ash, and smoke—
before I found me in my soft-petaled citrus, cinnamon
and pastels, fuschia and leather heels, la cosa con plumas.

Acknowledgments

Seattle Arts & Lectures: thank you for running the Seattle Youth Poet Laureate, Youth Poetry Fellowship, and Writers in the Schools programs—for not only believing that youth voices matter, but also for actively fostering and uplifting them. Having the experience as Seattle Youth Poet Laureate has been absolutely invaluable to me as a poet, performer, and all-around writer. Lastly, thank you for providing amazing poetry mentors and bringing fantastic authors to Seattle.

Urban Word NYC: thank you for starting the Youth Poet Laureate movement and giving a platform to so many incredible young poets and performers across the country. It was through the youth poet laureate movement that I saw how poetry can be used as a vehicle for social justice and a catalyst for change.

Poetry NW Editions, Abi Pollokoff, and Kevin Craft: thank you for your collaboration with Seattle Arts & Lectures on the Seattle Youth Poet Laureate series, and for your enduring generosity and kindness.

Auburn Arts Commission and Allison Hyde: thank you for the appointment of Auburn Poet Laureate and for giving me the opportunity to be a voice for poetry in Auburn and give back to the community that raised me. Thank you, Allison, for all your behind-the-scenes organizational sorcery.

Jourdan Imani Keith and Nanya Jhingran: thank you both for your invaluable insight and feedback, for your time and energy over these last few months, for helping me hone my craft, and for highlighting connections and recurring themes across my poems, the threads of this chapbook.

Susan Landgraf: thank you for facilitating the Teen Writer's Workshop at the Auburn Public Library, for teaching me to edit like a poet, and for showing me all the artistic possibilities. Thanks for exposing me to great poetry and giving me a standard to aspire to. Thanks for planting the seeds of poetry in me.

Rick Barot: thank you for all you taught me in Intro to Creative Writing and Intermediate Poetry, where the first drafts of "Ode to the Coyote," "Meditation on Belonging," "The Story of the Scar on My Left Knee," and "America Lives a Fantasy" were spun. Thanks for the lively poetic discussions and analyses, for giving us great readings, for guiding my work with an honest, enthusiastic hand, and for challenging me to become a better writer and to write what scares me. Thank you for exposing me to the work of so many fantastic writers.

Acknowledgments

Victoria Chang: I took *Dear Memory* with me on a two-week band trip to Ireland. It was the only book I brought, so I read it over and over on the long tour bus drives. When I went home I wrote "Dear Spanish" in one sitting. The poem remains essentially unchanged. In my book (pun intended), you are the master of the epistolary form. Thank you for gifting the world your poems. Thank you for inspiring me and so many others.

Jared: thanks for putting up with my poetry ramblings. Thank you for letting me force you to listen to me recite a poem I love, hate, or don't understand, so I can talk it through and evolve as a reader, a writer, and a thinker. Thanks for giving me feedback, even when I don't ask for it, don't like it, and get defensive. Thanks for cooking meals and doing laundry when I'm in a creative coma. Thanks for believing in me endlessly, telling me about the Seattle Youth Poet Laureate program, and encouraging me to apply, even when I didn't feel like I could call myself a poet.

Adam and Miri: thanks for being the best second pair of parents I could ever ask for and for taking me in. Adam, thanks for the coffee and conversation. I know way too much about sports now. I can only hope I'll use it for a book someday. Miri, thanks for the hugs, the popcorn, and the encouragement. Both of you are rays of sunshine in my life.

Mom: thank you for giving me a love of reading, writing, and libraries and for towing library books back and forth for the better part of two decades, not only for me but also for my siblings. Thanks for giving us the gift of words, of worlds, and all the paint.

Grey and Izzie: thank you for both for being your wonderful, bright selves, for breaking out of the mold, and for being the superstars you are.

Dad: Thanks for being my muse, my Spanish translator at times, for allowing me to interview you at ten p.m. at night, and for remaining somewhat of an enigma.

Notes

"America Lives a Fantasy" is an erasure from *Mr. Playboy: Mr. Hugh Hefner and the American Dream* by Steven Watts, published in 2008.

"My Father" is an erasure from a church service program. *Antiphon: Praise God in Song*, GIA Publications, 1979. *Verses: The Grail*, GIA Publications, 1963.

About the Author

Mateo Acuña is a Peruvian-American poet, writer, and visual artist who splits his time between Auburn and Seattle, Washington. He is the 2023–2024 Seattle Youth Poet Laureate and the 2024–2026 Auburn Poet Laureate, a SPOKES intern at Youth Speaks, a member of the Washington Arts Youth Leadership Cohort, and a librettist in the Seattle Opera Creation Lab. His and composer Mina Pariseau's opera, *Blood Dawn of the Inti Sun*, premiered at Tagney Jones Hall in 2024. He also sells jewelry made from repurposed and recycled materials.

This book is set in Futura PT and Bookmania

Book design by Cara Sutherland with assistance from
Indira Dahlstrom and Abi Pollokoff

Produced and published by Poetry NW Editions,
an educational press in the Written Arts Program
at Everett Community College

www.ingramcontent.com/pod-product-compliance
Lightning Source LLC
Chambersburg PA
CBHW052127070526
44586CB00016B/2126